Cover Art courtesy of

Marlén Laylah Gottman L. All rights reserved

All scripture quotations, unless otherwise indicated are taken
from the Holy Bible, King James Version.

ISBN: 978-1-300-85139-4

CHAPTER 1

INTRODUCTION

Over two millennia ago God stepped out of eternity became a man and dwelt among his people. He was born in humble circumstance, in a manger. He was not born to royalty but to ordinary people, to a man named Joseph, although Joseph was not his real father, and to a woman named Mary the wife of Joseph. He lived most of his life in obscurity being known as Jesus, the son of Joseph the carpenter in the town of Nazareth.

Jesus went to synagogue every Sabbath as was his custom and he observed the behavior of those he created. He grew, became strong and filled with wisdom even as a boy.

Once, when he was twelve years of age he missed his caravan back to Nazareth after the Passover and his family spent an entire day on the road before they noticed he was not with the caravan.

Returning to Jerusalem they searched for him for three days and on the third day they found him in the Temple court among the rabbis. He was not only attentively listening to what they were saying, but he was also asking some very good questions. So good in fact that everybody who heard him were astonished at his insight and responses, even the rabbis.

Jesus' parents were naturally upset with him, but his only response to them was that he had to be about his Father's business. He was of course not talking about carpentry.

For the next eighteen years or so Jesus remained the obedient and thoughtful son he had always been. He grew in both wisdom and stature and gained favor with men and with God.

This all changed in the fifteenth year of Emperor Tiberius' rule when Pontius Pilate was the governor of Judah and Herod was the ruler of Galilee.

John the son of Zacharias, Jesus' own cousin was called into the wilderness by God to preach the baptism of repentance for the remission of sins.

The Jewish people often asked John if he were the long awaited Messiah. He would tell those who asked that he indeed would baptize them in water, but that one mightier than he would come who would baptize them in the Holy Spirit and in fire.

Jesus came to his cousin John and was baptized. It was then that the Holy Spirit came down upon Jesus in physical form like a dove and a powerful voice boomed from heaven saying, ***"You are my Son, whom I love: I am well pleased with you." CJB Mark 1:11***

This voice was that of the King of the heavens and the King of the Earth. It was the voice of Him who walked with Adam in the garden. It was the same voice that told Abraham to leave all that was familiar to him and to travel to a far country and that his descendents would be as the sand of the seas or the stars in the heavens. This was the same voice that spoke to Moses on the mountain and gave Israel their great Covenant with God and it was the same voice who called John to the desert to baptize with water for the remission of sins.

When Jesus stepped out of the water, he stepped out of obscurity and into the greatest ministry that has ever been recorded in the annals of history.

For the next three years, Jesus went about his Father's business, teaching everyone he met about the Kingdom of His Father, the King.

Jesus was the greatest emissary that God had ever sent or would send to our world. He was

God's only son. He was directly in line for the throne. Jesus could see and hear clearly what his Father requested of him and he also knew the purpose for which he was sent to this place.

As is the case with any prince, they must first prove their worth by the trials that they face and the victories they achieve. Jesus faced many trials in his short three-year public appearance.

Jesus faced off with Satan in the wilderness and was victorious. He stared down demons and cast them out in Gadara. He healed people with incurable diseases and stood up to the mightiest religious leaders of his day.

Jesus proved his mastery over life by his immaculate birth. He proved his mastery over the Spiritual realm by his authority over the demons. He proved his mastery over the physical realm by his miracles. He proved his mastery over sin by his death on the cross and his mastery over death by his resurrection. He also proved to everyone who

would hear him the superiority of the Kingdom of
his Father over religion.

It has been more than two millennia since
Jesus went back to take his rightful place next to
the Father, yet the Kingdom of God today bears
little resemblance to the Kingdom of God that
Jesus taught us about. The people of God have
become contentious and argumentative. The word
of God has become a subject for debate and
ridicule and the people of God have abandoned all
pretense of holiness.

Denominationalism has divided the body
of Christ. Since debate breeds division, great
chasms have appeared in the Kingdom of God.

Counterfeits to true spirituality have
cropped up everywhere and the fields of faith are
choked with these weeds of false religion.

Dunes of compromise have covered the
Kingdom and our own shabby creations of religion
teeter on these shifting sands ready to collapse at
any moment.

Instead of advancing the Kingdom of God we have been in a slow retreat. Instead of standing up to the Goliaths in the world we shrink back and hope that they don't discover where we are hiding. Instead of acting like emissaries of the Prince we act like vagrants traveling from one inn to the next always with our hands extended asking for help.

Instead of ruling the world well, we seek to be well rid of the world. Stumbling around in the darkness as our lamps flicker and go out.

There are those though who have not bowed their knee to Baal, the prince of demons. There are those who even now labor to be ready when our King returns. There are those who shine in the darkness as beacons because they have always maintained full lamps as Jesus told us to do in his parable of the ten virgins.

It is time to step out of the mediocrity of religion and regain our rightful inheritance as subjects to the King of kings and Lord of lords. It is time to break the bonds of religious paradigms and free ourselves so that we can, in turn, free others. It is time to stop hiding in the winepress of religious convention and, though few in numbers stride forth to meet our destiny with swords in hand clad in the full armor of God.

CHAPTER 2

A REVOLUTION

This book is about change, but not the type of change our world leaders tell us about. This book is about exchanging our concept of "religion" for one of "Kingdom".

Jesus started this revolution over two thousand years ago when he taught his disciples, not about religion, but about the Kingdom of God.

It is the intent of this book to serve as a catalyst to produce a profound change in the way we perceive ourselves as Christians and how other people perceive those who follow Jesus and are called according to His name.

When a person becomes a "Christian" it seems a simple enough proposition at the time. Do you accept Jesus as your Lord or don't you? This decision was easy for me. Did I want to spend eternity with a loving Creator, or did I want to spend eternity in suffering and torment? Unfortunately this is where the easy decisions ended, at least until I discovered the truth about the Kingdom of God.

One day early in my Christian walk I asked my pastor, "What makes Christianity different from the other religions of the world?" and to this he responded and I paraphrase: Christianity is a relationship with God that in many ways takes the form of a religion.

This answer did little to answer my question and indeed raised many questions of it's own. What kind of a relationship was I to have with God I wondered? Was this relationship to be one of a servant to his master, or a tenant to his landlord? Was I supposed to treat God with great fear knowing that he could wipe me out of existence with but a thought, or was I supposed to treat God as a laughing best buddy who walked with me throughout life?

Furthermore, if this relationship was to take the form of a religion, then what denomination of Christianity was I to emulate? According to the Center for the Study of Global Christianity (CSGC) at Gordon-Conwell Theological Seminary, there are approximately 41,000 Christian denominations and organizations in the world.

I finally decided that I needed to go to a "Bible College" to learn more about the Bible and what God said about the matter. I considered both large established "accredited" institutions and smaller "non-accredited" Bible schools. I finally decided upon a non-denominational, non-accredited institute in Dallas Texas. The way I figured it, they would not be pushing their own agenda and would be focused more on the Word of God.

In 1989 I went to Bible school armed with a passage from Jeremiah.

Jeremiah 29:13 "And ye shall seek me, and find me, when ye shall search for me with all your heart."

It was during this time of separation and study of the Word that I began to realize that the accepted paradigm that people had concerning the Church was not at all what Jesus taught concerning his people.

During this time the Holy Spirit began to show me that Jesus never intended to start a new religion. The teachings that Jesus gave had nothing to do with religion. Jesus always taught "Kingdom".

To me this was foreign to everything I had ever been taught about my quote "Christian religion" unquote. This forced me into the revolutionary mindset of not seeing my faith in the Lord Jesus as just another religion, but rather, as a key component to my roles and responsibilities in the Kingdom of God.

Just as John the Baptist was a voice of one calling in the wilderness, prepare the way of the Lord: I believe that now is the time that we who follow the teachings of Jesus must by all means rise up and become a revolutionary force paving the way to the establishment of Jesus' Millennial Kingdom on the Earth physically based in Jerusalem.

We need to abandon the religious tyrants of the past and proceed with the truth that Jesus will soon return to set up His Kingdom. When he does return will He find any faithful among the living?

CHAPTER 3

KINGDOM NOT RELIGION

Jesus used the phrase "Kingdom of Heaven" thirty-one times in the book of Matthew alone and the phrase "Kingdom of God" is used by various people sixty-eight times in Matthew, Mark, Luke, John, Acts, Romans, I Corinthians, Galatians, Colossians, and II Thessalonians. The term "Kingdom" with no qualifier was used a further 10 times with "In my Father's Kingdom" being used once. Jesus always spoke of the Kingdom when relating God's plans for the Earth, not religion.

1 Samuel12:12 "And when ye saw that Nahash the King of the children of Ammon came against you, ye said unto me, Nay; but a king shall reign over us: when the Lord your God was your king."

In First Samuel when Nahash the King of the Ammonites was coming against them, the children of Israel came to the prophet Samuel and demanded a King be placed over them as was done by the other nations of the world.

The Lord God had protected the children of Israel for centuries. He was their rightful King, but the children of Israel feared and appointed a pretender to the throne rightfully held by God. Saul of the tribe of Benjamin was placed on the throne in approximately 1050 BC

The decision to appoint their own King led to much trouble and eventually divided the children of Israel into two Kingdoms in about 930 BC. One Kingdom was called Judah and the other Israel.

Israel had a string of Kings who went from bad to worse to abhorrent. Apart from the protection of God, Israel was the first of the divided Kingdoms to fall to their enemies.

Judah on the other hand had a number of Kings who were good and kept their hearts and their Kingdom turned towards God. Unfortunately this was but a handful of Kings out of many. The rest of Judah's Kings were bad, wicked or just downright evil.

In 597 BC the divided Kingdom fell when King Nebuchadnezzar of Babylon invaded Jerusalem.

Matthew 12:25 "And Jesus knew their thoughts, and said unto them, Every kingdom divided against itself is brought to desolation; and every city or house divided against itself shall not stand:"

Jesus well knew the plight of a house divided as he relates to us in the Gospel of Matthew.

One of the greatest adversaries to the Kingdom of God is religion. Religion only serves to deeply divide the body of Christ. This weakens the body and promotes disunity. A body broken into pieces cannot function very well and will soon die.

Acts 11:26 "And when he had found him, he brought him unto Antioch. And it came to pass, that a whole year they assembled themselves with the church, and taught much people. And the disciples were called Christians first in Antioch."

It was not long after Jesus went to be with the Father that the world started labeling the people who followed the teachings of Jesus as 'Christians'. Until then they had only thought of themselves as disciples. This happened in the city of Antioch as the previous verse relates.

It was not long until these 'Christians' as the world called them began to organize and before long in 313 AD the Roman Emperor

Constantine adopted Christianity as the official religion of Rome.

Until the formalization of Christianity as an organized religion, believers would meet in one another's homes as the leadership went from city to city visiting and building up the believers in their faith in their home based groups.

These home groups served to decentralize the early church and made it that much more difficult for the enemies of Christ to root out and to destroy it.

The ministries of Apostle, Prophet, Evangelist, Pastor and Teacher would itinerate through the home groups and build up the body of Christ teaching believers about the Kingdom of God.

1 Corinthians 1:11-13 "For it hath been declared unto me of you, my brethren, by them which are of the house of Chloe, that there are contentions among you. Now this I say, that every one of you saith, I am of Paul; and I of

Apollos; and I of Cephas; and I of Christ. Is Christ divided? was Paul crucified for you? or were ye baptized in the name of Paul?"

In the days of the Apostles fractures started forming in the body of Christ as people took their eyes off of their King (Jesus) and started gazing intently on His servants, comparing one servant to another.

Paul was pleading with the body of Christ to keep their eyes on Jesus, the author and finisher of our faith.

As we have mentioned before, Jesus told us that a house divided couldn't stand. As these divisions occurred, wicked men would step in and lead the people astray creating even deeper rifts and eventually denominations arose, each with a slightly different statement of faith, as the body of Christ was slowly torn apart over the course of centuries.

It is not altogether true that Jesus did not speak about religion. Jesus did discuss religion with his disciples, but not in the way that you may think. When Jesus spoke of religion it was in condemnation to what the Scribes and Pharisees had done to the truth.

The Scribes and the Pharisees had used the truth of God to build their own religious strongholds in which they kept their adherents captive. These religions served to enslave men to their doctrines and used the truth only to promote their own selfish agendas.

In the Book of Revelation, Babylon the Great the Mother of Harlots is used to illustrate those who would use the truth to build their own empires.

Revelation 17:5-6, "And upon her forehead was a name written, MYSTERY, BABYLON THE GREAT, THE MOTHER OF HARLOTS AND ABOMINATIONS OF THE EARTH. And I saw the woman drunken with the blood of the saints, and with the blood of the martyrs of

Jesus: and when I saw her, I wondered with great admiration."

Just like Mystery Babylon, these religions may have many beautiful trappings on the outside with gold and purple and golden cups and beautiful buildings, but on the inside they have been made drunk by the power they receive from all those who follow after them.

Those thrust into leadership by the complacent masses have many times become lazy gaining their support from the multitude of people that flock to them to be fed. The altars in their houses of worship have been replaced by stages and their songs have changed their focus from God to self in an effort to keep the people coming back for more.

Some of these leaders have even usurped the Holy Spirit, by insisting that only they can hear correctly from the Lord. This in turn gives their followers an excuse not to search for the truth on their own and so they get fat off of the spoon-fed pre-processed sermons they receive once a week.

These phony leaders make themselves rich by the donations of those who are told that their money will go towards building this project or that project. They keep their flocks at home by disseminating gossip about other religious structures. They have become a democracy instead of a Theocracy. Church boards have replaced the five-fold ministry. They rely on "consensus" rather than the "constant sense" of what the Holy Spirit wants to do and where He wants to go.

Simon Peter describes these false leaders as follows.

2 Peter 2:17-18 "17 Waterless springs they are, mists driven by a gust of wind; for them has been reserved the blackest darkness. Mouthing grandiosities of nothingness, they play on the desires of the old nature, in order to seduce with debaucheries people who have just begun to escape from those whose way of life is wrong." CJB

In Revelation 18:13 when describing the items that Babylon the Great traded for the list includes one odd item. It states that Babylon also traded in the *"...souls of men."*

God will judge Babylon and Babylon represents an apostate, idolatrous, religious system that uses the truth contained in the word of God to sway people away from what Jesus taught. What was it that Jesus taught us you ask? Jesus taught us about the Kingdom of God.

In truth there are many religions on the face of the earth, even so I submit that there are but two Kingdoms. There exists the Kingdom of light and the Kingdom of darkness only.

The Word of God is replete with instances where God contrasts two things by demonstrating polar opposites. God shows us darkness, and then creates light. God shows us wickedness then demonstrates righteousness and God has told us that when we die, we will live eternally in one of two places, heaven or hell.

I would like to take some time to discuss three such contrasts that the Word of God makes.

The first contrast is between two Kingdoms; one of darkness and the other of light. The second contrast is between two covenants; one of judgment and the other of grace. The third contrast is between two men, the Old Man and the New Man.

CHAPTER 4

TWO KINGDOMS

1 John 1:5-7 "This then is the message which we have heard of him, and declare unto you, that God is light, and in him is no darkness at all. If we say that we have fellowship with him, and walk in darkness, we lie, and do not the truth: But if we walk in the light, as he is in the light, we have fellowship one with another, and the blood of Jesus Christ his Son cleanseth us from all sin."

As my perception of the Kingdom of God cleared, I soon realized that there were but two Kingdoms at work in this world. There was the Kingdom of Light ruled by God and alternatively there was the Kingdom of darkness ruled by the prince of darkness. Either you were a subject of the one, or you were by default a subject of the other. Either you walked boldly in the light, or you would stumble around in the darkness.

A subject is a person who is a member of a Kingdom and as such has a King. Each Kingdom, both darkness and light, have subjects. The subjects of the Kingdom of darkness are often called by a variety of names such as unrighteous, sinners, old man and wicked and so on.

On the other hand the subjects of the Kingdom of light are also known by many names that include righteous, redeemed, born again, believers and the Church among other names.

For now, let us discuss the Greek word that is translated "Church" in our Bibles. This word is Ekklesia and literally means called out or called forth.

The term Ekklesia is really quite descriptive of those who follow after the Lord

Jesus Christ for we are called out of the Kingdom of Darkness and into the Kingdom of Light. The Apostle Peter describes the church in the following way.

> ***1 Peter 2:9 "But ye are a chosen generation, a royal priesthood, an holy nation, a peculiar people; that ye should shew forth the praises of him who hath called you out of darkness into his marvellous light;"***

God has called us out of the darkness, and pleads with us to come over to his Kingdom. He calls us to him to be a peculiar people. We should seem odd to those who are in the world. When they look at our lives they should be perplexed for the things of the Spirit seem like foolishness to them who are perishing.

We are called to be a holy, or set apart nation. Again, we are not talking about being religious; we are talking about a geo-political entity called the Kingdom of God. The term "nation" here is ethnos in the Greek where we get our word Ethnic and it refers to a people group and not a nationality.

This verse in First Peter also calls us a royal priesthood. The priesthood is that people group who demonstrate in our lives God's Kingdom on the earth until the return of the King.

Finally we are a chosen generation, the Greek here being elektos meaning that we were elected. We do not become members of the Kingdom randomly, but by the divine election of our God and King.

Jesus is beseeching us to come into the light. He sees us in our fearful plight and calls with his hand outstretched saying, *"Come, ye blessed of my Father, inherit the kingdom prepared for you from the foundation of the world:" Matthew 25:34*

Darkness can be overwhelming, frightening and, well, just downright scary. Even so, darkness, in itself is nothing; or rather it is the absence of something. The something I am speaking about is 'light' and when God created the 'light', then 'darkness' disappeared. Darkness is nothing more than the absence of light.

John 8:12 "Then spake Jesus again unto them, saying, I am the light of the world: he that followeth me shall not walk in darkness, but shall have the light of life."

Spiritual darkness in the same way is the lack of something vital. Jesus tells us that He is the light of the world and that walking after Him will dispel the darkness so prevalent in the world.

What is this "light of life" that Jesus speaks about? In the opening remarks of his Gospel, the Apostle John gives us some insight to the back-story of Jesus and why He was able above all men to call Himself the light of the World.

John 1:1-5 "In the beginning was the Word, and the Word was with God, and the Word was God. The same was in the beginning with God. All things were made by him; and without him was not any thing made that was made. In him was life; and the life was the light of men. And the light shineth in darkness; and the darkness comprehended it not."

And again speaking of Jesus in his letter to the Colossians the Apostle Paul states the following.

Colossians 1:16 "For by him were all things created, that are in heaven, and that are in earth, visible and invisible, whether they be thrones, or dominions, or principalities, or powers: all things were created by him, and for him:"

The Apostle John is stating that Jesus was also known as the Word and that Jesus was present with God in the beginning. "The Word was with God, and the Word was God".

John and Paul both confirm that Jesus created all things both visible and invisible. The Apostle John goes on to state that to as many as do receive Jesus as their Lord, to them he gave the power to become the sons of God. These are those people who believe on the name of Jesus and who are born of the Spirit of God.

Jesus does this by the power of the Holy Spirit and a process of rebirth.

The decision to be born-again belongs to us and we alone can make it. It is not until we are born-again that we can enter into the Kingdom of God.

Romans 10:9 "That if thou shalt confess with thy mouth the Lord Jesus, and shalt believe in thine heart that God hath raised him from the dead, thou shalt be saved."

It is we who must do the confessing, and it is with our mouths that we do confess. You can't cheat and say, well God knows my heart and never confess your faith. It is also with our hearts that we believe that Jesus conquered death and are saved. It takes both a verbal confession of faith and a heartfelt belief in resurrection to be saved and enter into the Kingdom of God.

The name of Jesus in the Hebrew tongue
is Yeshua. The name Yeshua literally means
"salvation". Jesus is our salvation when we are lost
and alone in the Kingdom of darkness.

Put yourself in the place of a child, lost in
the dark woods. Those who have been lost and
alone in the dark understand how important light
is to their salvation.

You may be able to hear voices calling to
you from the dark, but to follow after these echoes
can lead you astray or even over a precipice.

Then you see it, a light shining in the
darkness. You now have a destination to strive for.
Step by step you carefully make your way towards
the light. Having no light of your own many times
you stumble and fall. You call out for help and the
rescuer hears your voice. His light now shines in
your direction and he sees you. He tells you to stay
where you are at because you cannot see the sheer
plunge that is at your feet. Before you know it, he
is at your side and you are rescued.

Matthew 4:16 " the people living in darkness have seen a great light; upon those living in the region, in the shadow of death, light has dawned." CJB

This is how Jesus rescues us. We see His light and we call out to Him. He hears our voice and he comes to us faster than we can imagine. We are saved and He walks with us to lead us to safety. He covers us with his own coat and heals our wounds.

God calls every man and woman ever born to walk with him in the Kingdom of light. God loves us so much that He descended from on high into our dark world to act as a beacon to draw all men to the Kingdom of His Father.

The Kingdom is constantly advancing and Jesus is always on the move. Once we have been rescued, covered and cured, that is but the beginning of our walk with our King. We must continue to follow him for the rest of our lives in order to remain in his light. Jesus told us that He was the Light of the world and that if we would follow him then we would walk in the light and not in the darkness.

After salvation comes a decision. Do we choose to follow after Jesus and remain in the light, or do we wander off again into the darkness to try to make our own way.

This decision will affect the rest of our lives and God will not coerce us either one way or the other. He leaves the decision up to us.

God's desire is to have subjects who willingly follow him. We can choose to remain faithful to the Lord, or we can choose to walk back into the Kingdom of darkness. This is a decision we will face every day for the rest of our lives. Joshua gives his people the following challenge prior to entering the Promised Land.

Joshua 24:15 "And if it seem evil unto you to serve the Lord, choose you this day whom ye will serve; whether the gods which your fathers served that were on the other side of the

flood, or the gods of the Amorites, in whose land
ye dwell: but as for me and my house, we will
serve the Lord."

Notice that Joshua exhorts the people
"choose you this day". Every morning when you
wake up you will have to choose to serve the Lord,
or choose to walk after your own selfish desires.

In the beginning it will be difficult not to
fall into the old habits and routines, which became
so familiar to us in the darkness. Like a blind
person who just receives their sight, it is easy to
walk the old paths.

A person who is blind relies on routine
and habit in order to do anything. The furniture
has to be in certain places, and when eating the
utensils have to be at specific locations. The food
on the plate needs also to be served in the same
way every day.

A blind person can appear quite
independent as long as their routine is not
interrupted. If you move one piece of furniture or

one item on the table they are back to groping around in the dark.

Even so, when a person submits to the rule of Jesus in their lives, then things are going to change. The ways of darkness do not function in the Kingdom of Light.

John 1:5 "And the light shineth in the darkness; and the darkness comprehended it not."

If you try to function in the Kingdom of Light by using the tools of darkness, then you will fail. In the book of Ephesians Paul warns us.

Ephesians 5:6-8 "Let no man deceive you with vain words: for because of these things cometh the wrath of God upon the children of disobedience. Be not ye therefore partakers with them. For ye were sometimes darkness, but now are ye light in the Lord: walk as children of light:"

In 2 Corinthians 10:5 we are told to cast down *"imaginations, and every high thing that exalteth itself against the knowledge of God"* and we are further instructed in the same breath to bring *"into captivity every thought to the obedience of Christ;"*

Paul well knew the following passage from Isaiah. This passage illustrates how unrighteous thoughts can lead to wicked ways and that these thoughts and ways were not the way of the Kingdom of Light.

Isaiah 55:6-9 "Seek ye the Lord while he may be found, call ye upon him while he is near: Let the wicked forsake his way, and the unrighteous man his thoughts: and let him return unto the Lord, and he will have mercy upon him; and to our God, for he will abundantly pardon. For my thoughts are not your thoughts, neither are your ways my ways, saith the Lord. For as the heavens are higher than the earth, so are my ways higher than your ways, and my thoughts than your thoughts."

There will come a time when people will search for the Lord and they will not find him. He will withdraw his Holy Spirit from the earth. The time of grace will come to an end.

Rejoice those who are subjects of our King, for we have been rescued from the power of darkness and brought into the Kingdom of Light! Do not be confused by the multitude of religions and faiths prevalent in the world today.

The truth is simple. There are but two Kingdoms, one of darkness and the other of light. Learn of, and walk in the ways of our King, Jesus, and you will be a part of the Kingdom of Light.

Colossians 1:12-13 "Giving thanks unto the Father, which hath made us meet to be partakers of the inheritance of the saints in light: Who hath delivered us from the power of darkness, and hath translated us into the kingdom of his dear Son:"

CHAPTER 5

TWO COVENANTS

The most common greeting in the world, the handshake, is derived from covenant. In times past when two tribes or families would bind together they would cut each other's right arm above the wrist and allow the blood flow down to mingle in their palms as they grasped hands.

From that point forward when two tribes would meet their leaders would offer each other their right hands and thus display the scars they acquired from prior covenants they had cut. The more scars someone had, the stronger that tribe was.

A blood covenant was taken so seriously that when one tribe was in a covenant relationship with a second tribe and the first tribe was attacked, then the second tribe would come to the defense of their covenant brother and lay down their lives if necessary.

A shedding of blood is necessary for any covenant to be binding. Also a shedding of blood is necessary to forgive sin.

Hebrews 9:22 "In fact, according to the Torah, almost everything is purified with blood; indeed, without the shedding of blood there is no forgiveness of sins." CJB

Jesus laid down his own life for us for the remission of sins as he spoke about at the last supper just before his crucifixion.

Matthew 26:28 "For this is my blood, which ratifies the New Covenant, my blood shed on behalf of many, so that they may have their sins forgiven." CJB

I would like to speak now of two covenants that God has made with man. The first covenant I would speak of was delivered to Moses on mount Sinai and was ratified by the blood of animals. This covenant we know commonly as "the Law".

The second great covenant was delivered by God to man in the person of Jesus Christ and is ratified with Jesus' own blood. This covenant we refer to as the new covenant.

Hebrews 8:8 "For God does find fault with the people when he says, "'See! The days are coming,' says ADONAI, 'when I will establish over the house of Isra'el and over the house of Y'hudah a new covenant." CJB

The term "*Covenant*" in the Greek and Hebrew is many times translated as "*Testament*", such as in the "Old *Testament*" and the "*New Testament*". The Bible records both Old Covenant and New Covenant.

People often mistake a covenant with a promise. A promise is not a binding agreement whereas a covenant is a binding agreement. Merriam Webster defines the word Covenant as *"a formal, solemn, and binding agreement"* and again *"a written agreement or promise usually under seal between two or more parties especially for the performance of some action."*

The covenant that the Bible speaks of is a form of Blood covenant and is sealed with blood. The blood makes the Covenant binding.

In the Old Testament the covenant was renewed each year with the blood of animals, but the new Covenant, which is sealed by the blood of Jesus Christ, is an eternal Covenant.

When we come together as should be done regularly, we are to partake of bread and wine in what is called "communion" or the "Lords Supper". We do this in remembrance of the new covenant sealed with the blood of Jesus. It is by the blood of Jesus, represented by the wine, that we have forgiveness of sin, and it is by the body of Jesus, represented by the bread, that we walk in divine health, for by His stripes we were healed.

Isaiah 53:5 "But he was wounded for our transgressions, he was bruised for our iniquities: the chastisement of our peace was upon him; and with his stripes we are healed."

This Blood Covenant sealed with the blood of Jesus is the binding contract that all of those who are subjects of the Kingdom of God fall under. This contract binds King and Subject to the performance of certain actions. The action performed by the King is found in the book of Hebrews and is that of eternal redemption.

Hebrews 9:12 "he entered the Holiest Place once and for all. And he entered not by means of the blood of goats and calves, but by means of his own blood, thus setting people free forever." CJB

In other words, the price that was paid to redeem, or purchase, us was paid with His own blood while he hung on the cross suffering and dying for us.

Covenants are always two sided, so we also have a part to play if this covenant is to be valid. As a subject to our King we are bound by this covenant sealed with the blood of Jesus to do nothing less than exactly what our King wills.

Hebrews 10:36 " For you need to hold out; so that, by having done what God wills, you may receive what he has promised." CJB

You may be asking yourself, "How am I to know what my King wills if He is not here to communicate his will to me?"

The answer to this is that our King may be at the right hand of the Father in heaven, but He has set in his place a regent. A regent is a person who governs a Kingdom in the absence of the sovereign. Jesus set up a regent here on the earth and that regent is none other than the Holy Spirit.

It is by the Spirit of God that we know the will of God. It is by the Spirit of God that we can correctly interpret the word of truth. It is by the Spirit of God that we know what things please and displease our King.

The Holy Spirit is the conduit that transfers the commands of heaven to us here on the earth. He knows the mind of the Father and Son because he is the third part of our Triune God. Jesus, the Father and the Spirit are one.

There are many false regents who set themselves up to speak on behalf of our King. They tell those who mistakenly follow them that only they can hear correctly from the King. They might also say that the Bible is correct only in as much as it is interpreted correctly. These are religious pretenders, of whom our King will pass the following judgment.

Matthew 7:23 "I never knew you: depart from me, ye that work iniquity."

There is no theologian better equipped to correctly interpret the Word of God than the Holy Spirit who is in constant contact with the Father and the Son.

It is the Holy Spirit who quickens the word to us and helps us apply the Word to our daily lives.

The Holy Spirit was sent by Jesus to fulfill the vital purpose of changing a believer from the inside out.

John 14:16-17 "And I will pray the Father, and he shall give you another Comforter, that he may abide with you for ever; Even the Spirit of truth; whom the world cannot receive, because it seeth him not, neither knoweth him: but ye know him; for he dwelleth with you, and shall be in you."

CHAPTER 6

TWO MEN

Religion teaches that there is a lot of grey in the world, but in keeping with our ongoing discussion of polar opposites I would again like to point out that there is only light and darkness. Grey is simply the result of mixing darkness with the light and as I mentioned before, the two are not compatible.

Any Kingdom has a King and it has territory and it has subjects. As subjects to the Kingdom of God we are also subject to the rules of the Kingdom. These rules include the Law of the first covenant, which Jesus summed up simply by giving the following instruction.

Matthew 12:28-31 "And one of the scribes came, and having heard them reasoning together, and perceiving that he had answered them well, asked him, Which is the first commandment of all? And Jesus answered him, The first of all the commandments is, Hear, O Israel; The Lord our God is one Lord: And thou shalt love the Lord thy God with all thy heart, and with all thy soul, and with all thy mind, and with all thy strength: this is the first commandment. And the second is like, namely this, Thou shalt love thy neighbour as thyself. There is none other commandment greater than these."

Once again the foolish scribes were trying to trick Jesus into saying something that they could condemn him for.

Knowing their intentions, Jesus told them that they were to first Love the Lord with all their heart, soul and mind and then they were to love their neighbors as themselves.

If we who follow the teachings of Jesus Christ would but follow these two commands, then keeping the rest of the Law would not be a problem. The problem arises when we are enticed away from these two simple instructions by our own lusts.

John 3:5 "Jesus answered, Verily, verily, I say unto thee, Except a man be born of water and of the Spirit, he cannot enter into the Kingdom of God."

The way we announce to the world that we are changing Kingdoms is through the observation of baptism. Jesus told us that we needed both Baptism in water and baptism in the Spirit to overcome the old man.

Baptism represents the death and burial of the old man and the rebirth or resurrection of a new creation. In this way we give notice to the world that we are following a new leader. It is the Holy Spirit who leads us in the resurrected

overcoming life that a follower of Jesus Christ
enjoys.

**2 Corinthians 5:17 "Therefore if any
man be in Christ, he is a new creature: old
things are passed away; behold, all things are
become new."**

The Apostle Paul uses the term "the old
man" to describe a person prior to their
acceptance into the Kingdom and inclusion in the
new Covenant.

Other phrases used to describe the old
man are the body of sin, the flesh, the sinful
nature, the wicked, and the unrighteous to name a
few.

A wonderful benefit of living under the
New Covenant is that we are no longer compelled
to sin because the Holy Spirit leads us in all truth.

Sin is defined here as doing that which
displeases our King. The Holy Spirit was sent by

Jesus to fulfill a vital purpose in a believer's life. This purpose is to lead us in all truth.

The Holy Spirit works on us from the inside out. He knows our thoughts and intentions and guides us in the ways that please our King.

We are bound by our own words when we confessed that Jesus is Lord and through the observation of baptism to do those things that please our King. To do something that displeases our King is to sin.

As I have said, it is by the Holy Spirit that we know those things that please our King and those things that do not. Also, as I said in the chapter "Two Kingdoms", the tools of darkness will not work in the Kingdom of light, yet many people persist in their ruinous thinking that leads to wicked actions and thus continue in lives that are displeasing to our King.

The apostle Paul well knew this struggle as he relates in the following passage.

Romans 7:18-19, " For I know that in me (that is, in my flesh,) dwelleth no good thing: for to will is present with me; but how to perform that which is good I find not. For the good that I would I do not: but the evil which I would not, that I do."

The Complete Jewish Bible relates the verse this way.

Romans 7:18-19 "For I know that there is nothing good housed inside me - that is, inside my old nature. I can want what is good, but I can't do it! For I don't do the good I want; instead, the evil that I don't want is what I do!"

Paul went on to lament in ***Romans 7:24 "O wretched man that I am! who shall deliver me from the body of this death?" CJB***

The answer to Paul's query "Who will deliver me from the body of this death?" comes quickly in the very next chapter when the Apostle Paul triumphantly proclaims that there is no condemnation as a subject of Jesus' Kingdom if two things are observed. First we must not walk after the flesh, and second we must walk after the Spirit.

Romans 8:1 "There is therefore now no condemnation to them which are in Christ Jesus, who walk not after the flesh, but after the Spirit. For the law of the Spirit of life in Christ Jesus hath made me free from the law of sin and death. For what the law could not do, in that it was weak through the flesh, God sending his own Son in the likeness of sinful flesh, and for sin, condemned sin in the flesh: That the righteousness of the law might be fulfilled in us, who walk not after the flesh, but after the Spirit."

It is the Spirit of God who frees us from the old man. It is by the Spirit of God that we can live a life that is pleasing to the King.

As I have mentioned, God loves to show contrasts in His Word. Another such contrast is that between the fruit of the spirit and the fruit of the sinful nature.

The new creation bears the fruit of the Spirit as mentioned in Galatians chapter five as a natural outgrowth from their life in Christ Jesus. This fruit includes love, joy, peace, patience, kindness, goodness, faithfulness, humility and self-control.

By contrast, it is obvious if a person is bearing the fruit of the sinful nature. The Apostle Paul, in the complete Jewish Bible, describes this rotten and stinking fruit.

Galatians 5:19-21 "And it is perfectly evident what the old nature does. It expresses itself in sexual immorality, impurity and indecency; involvement with the occult and with drugs; in feuding, fighting, becoming jealous and getting angry; in selfish ambition, factionalism, intrigue and envy; in drunkenness, orgies and things like these. I warn you now as I have warned you before: those who do such things will have no share in the Kingdom of God!" CJB

Every day we must wake up and decide that we will follow the leading of the Holy Spirit. The Holy Spirit is always there to guide and direct you. We must not only listen intently, but we must also do that which the Holy Spirit encourages us to do. It is only the Holy Spirit that can graft the word of God in our hearts to eventually become a part of who we are.

When I was a kid we planted a walnut tree in our front yard. The tree was called a black walnut tree and usually put out small nuts that had a nasty black shell that were not good for much of anything.

After a few weeks, once the tree became rooted in the soil, my grandfather came over and cut off the top of the tree and split the slender trunk down the middle. I thought he had killed the tree, but he had brought with him a cutting from an English walnut. English walnuts are wonderful!

They are large and have lots of meat and are easy to shell.

My grandfather then trimmed the end of the English walnut cutting and placed it in the notch of the split walnut base. After he did this he wrapped the trunk in cloth and melted wax that would act as a bandage keeping out disease and pests while the tree healed.

I asked him why he did this and he told me that the black walnut has good roots and will not rot in moist weather. The English walnut by contrast needs dry ground and its roots will rot with too much rain. The combination of the two would make a tree that was much stronger. Even to this day that tree stands and it is obvious where the Black walnut trunk ends and the English walnut begins.

In the same way, the Holy Spirit has the unique ability to graft the Word of God into a believer's heart. This makes a person much more resilient to the temptations or afflictions of this world. Eventually the Word becomes a part of you and you do not struggle with the same sins over and over again as you grow and become one with the word.

CHAPTER 7

KINGDOM PARADIGM

Thomas Kuhn coined the term "paradigm shift" in 1962 in his book "The Structure of Scientific Revolutions". On page ten Kuhn argues that scientific advancement does not happen by a gradual increase, but rather is a *"series of peaceful interludes punctuated by intellectually violent revolutions"*, and in those revolutions *"one conceptual world view is replaced by another"*.

In the same way, I believe that the body of Christ is quickly approaching just such a violent revolution where a new understanding of the body of Christ will replace our current concept of the Church. This will happen when the Church,

Ecclesia, stops seeing ourselves as merely one of many religions, but as a Kingdom of light ruled by a King confronting another Kingdom, one of darkness, ruled by the prince of darkness.

This confrontation will culminate in a great battle that is waged between the forces of darkness and the forces of the Light. This battle will take place in a location called in the Hebrew tongue Armageddon. Revelation 16:16

Even though most people view Christianity as a religion and not a Kingdom. This is not what Jesus taught us. Jesus taught us that we were subjects of The Kingdom of God. Religion might have a small place in the Kingdom of God, but the Kingdom of God is so immeasurably huge that it cannot possibly be contained in a religious paradigm.

The Kingdom of God is vast having its source in the very beginning when God created the universe. Since God created the entire universe He is the rightful possessor of all the planets, stars and galaxies therein by right of this same creative act.

The subjects of the Kingdom of God number in the trillions. All those who have gone before and all those alive today and all those who will accept Jesus as their Savior in the future belong to the Kingdom of God.

The Kingdom of God includes all those who have confessed or who will confess that Jesus is their Lord and believe that God raised him from the dead on the third day. This also includes all of those Jesus ministered to when he was in the grave for three days, that is, those who lived and died on the earth prior to His arrival.

The Kingdom of God is eternal and will never come to an end. Deep calls out to deep and our eternal spirits seek a place in which to spend eternity. God created his Kingdom to meet this need and nothing man has created can ever come close to what God has already created.

When one starts to comprehend the vastness of the Kingdom of God it is easy to feel insignificant, but this simply is not so. The Apostle Paul taught us that we were all members of one body and as such are a vital albeit small part of a much larger whole.

Ephesians 4:15-16 "But speaking the truth in love, may grow up into him in all things, which is the head, even Christ: From whom the whole body fitly joined together and compacted by that which every joint supplieth, according to the effectual working in the measure of every part, maketh increase of the body unto the edifying of itself in love."

The concept of being a small part of a larger body is seen in Romans chapter twelve and First Corinthians chapter twelve, as well as in Ephesians chapter four where the Bible speaks of all believers being a part of the body of Christ.

Also in Ephesians chapters four and five as well as in First Corinthians chapter eleven the

Bible speaks of Jesus being the Head of the body.

When talking to his spiritual son Timothy the Apostle Paul states the following.

2 Timothy 3:16-17 "16 All scripture is given by inspiration of God, and is profitable for doctrine, for reproof, for correction, for instruction in righteousness: That the man of God may be perfect, thoroughly furnished unto all good works."

It is from the head that instructions are relayed to the entire body. It is not up to the body to decide on a direction that the head has not conceived and a body without a head is dead.

To continue the illustration, the head (brain) is connected to the body through the central nervous system, which is nothing more than an extension of the brain itself. The central nervous system receives instruction from the head (brain) and relays this instruction to all of the members of the body.

In this illustration the Holy Spirit is representative of the nervous system that controls every function of the body. Just as the nervous system infiltrates every part of the human body, down to the smallest of cells, it is the Holy Spirit who dwells in the hearts of every believer. It is the Holy Spirit who relays the plans of God to His body and it is only by the Holy Spirit that we can fulfill the vision that comes from the eyes, through the brain as well.

There are those in this world who have sought to replace the work of the Holy Spirit with their own particular religion or denomination. The debate this produces breeds division in the body of Christ and these divisions seriously injure the work of God in the world.

Dogma and belief statements have fractured the body of Christ and served to usurp a direct connection with God for every believer through the Holy Spirit. These religious pretenders assert that only certain people can hear from God correctly and that only certain people can interpret the word of God correctly and only certain people can see what God is doing in the world correctly.

This type of domineering religious structure acts like a rigid cast and paralyzes the body of Christ as effectively as a fractured or broken spine will paralyze the human body.

The religions and denominations of the world contain myriads of people unable to move because they are bound by religious rules and regulations that govern almost every aspect of their lives. These regulations act like the strings that bound Gulliver after the Lilliputians had tied him down. Each string was not difficult to break individually, but the sheer number of them held him in place and bound him tightly.

These people may indeed be spiritual giants ready to go forth and battle on behalf of the Kingdom of God, but they find themselves unable to do so because of the all the strings religious organizations attached to them.

Matthew 23:1-3 "Then spake Jesus to the multitude, and to his disciples, Saying The scribes and the Pharisees sit in Moses' seat: All therefore whatsoever they bid you observe, that observe and do; but do not ye after their works: for they say, and do not."

Without the direction of the Holy Spirit necessary to help the individual to lead a holy life; religion alone produces nothing but hypocrites, as was the case with the Pharisees of Jesus' time.

Luke 20:27 27 "Then came to him certain of the Sadducees, which deny that there is any resurrection; and they asked him,"

Without the empowerment of the Holy Spirit religion can never conceive of the supernatural power of God because of their adherence to religious rules and regulations, as was the case with the Sadducees of Jesus' time that refused to believe in a literal resurrection. It simply did not fit within their religious paradigm.

We must free ourselves from the paralyzing effects of religion and adopt a Kingdom paradigm that brings with itself the life that issues from a direct connection to the head of the Church, Jesus Christ, through the Holy Spirit.

I Timothy 6:14-15 "That thou keep this commandment without spot, unrebukable, until the appearing of our Lord Jesus Christ: Which in his times he shall shew, who is the blessed and only Potentate, the King of kings, and Lord of lords;"

In First Timothy the Apostle Paul describes Jesus as the blessed and only Potentate. As I mentioned before, we are each a small and vital element of a larger Kingdom. If we are a part of a Kingdom, then there must be a King. As we have discussed, Jesus is the Head of the Church and it is upon the head that the royal emblem, the crown, resides.

Revelation 17:14 "These shall make war with the Lamb, and the Lamb shall overcome them: for he is Lord of lords, and King of kings: and they that are with him are called, and chosen, and faithful."

In Revelation describing the battle of Armageddon the Apostle John describes Jesus as King of kings and Lord of lords.

Revelation 19:16 "And he hath on his vesture and on his thigh a name written, KING OF KINGS, AND LORD OF LORDS."

And again in Revelation 19 when Jesus returns to set up his physical Kingdom based in Jerusalem John describes Him as King of kings and Lord of lords.

It is Jesus who is the sole legal heir to God's Kingdom and it is Jesus who is our rightful King.

We as subjects of the Kingdom of God must stop seeing ourselves as members of any particular religion. The idea of membership in itself is flawed. Membership as in the case with country clubs and department stores is something we have control over and we can rescind our membership at any time, as we desire.

It is our decision to accept Jesus as Lord, and this decision makes us His subjects. At that point we can enjoy the protection and blessings of His Kingdom as long as we walk in the light, meaning under His authority and obeying His precepts.

As I have mentioned before, Jesus did not come to teach us a new and better religion. Jesus came and showed us a new and better Kingdom. This Kingdom is established forever and is ruled by the wisest and most powerful person who was ever born. That person is our Lord and King, Jesus the Messiah.

CHAPTER 8

KINGDOM ME

John 5:42 "But I know you, that ye have not the love of God in you."

When ministering in Utah, we would occasionally experience what were called temperature inversions. During these times cold air would settle into the valleys, while warmer air rode over the colder air providing a cap of sorts.

These temperature inversions could last for weeks and over time the air would become more and more saturated with pollutants. At times public warnings were issued not to drive or operate machinery unless absolutely necessary. These temperature inversions led to all sorts of respiratory ailments and many became sick because of the pollution in the air.

During the initial phases of a temperature inversion the skies are clear and the wind is calm but the temperature is cold. At first you can see the mountains in the distance rising majestically against the blue sky. As time goes on and the pollution index rises, the sky turns a grey color and the mountains become barely discernable in the distance as the pollution builds and builds.

The only thing that can break a temperature inversion is a storm. A strong wind is needed to blow into the area and mix the colder and warmer layers of air so that the trapped pollutants can be released. If the storm is not strong enough then the inversion layer remains and conditions become worse and then people can die from any number of respiratory ailments.

Matthew 24:12 "And because iniquity shall abound, the love of many shall wax cold."

The Kingdom of God can also experience what amounts to a spiritual temperature inversion. This happens when the hearts of believers turn cold and the love of God departs from the hearts of His subjects.

Our prayers and worship are designed to pierce the heavens and rise to the throne of God. Jesus, when speaking of the last days warned us against becoming cold and unloving.

1 Corinthians 13:1-3 NAS "If I speak with the tongues of men and of angels, but do not have love, I have become a noisy gong or a clanging cymbal. If I have the gift of prophecy, and know all mysteries and all knowledge; and if I have all faith, so as to remove mountains, but do not have love, I am nothing. And if I give all my possessions to feed the poor, and if I surrender my body to be burned, but do not have love, it profits me nothing."

It would be easy to turn from a wicked world and focus solely on our personal relationship with the Lord, but without love, what are we? Paul told the Corinthian believers in the above verse that those who do great works without love motivating them are nothing more than self-important bags of hot air.

John 13:35 "By this shall all men know that ye are my disciples, if ye have love one to another."

Jesus told us that there was one thing that set subjects of the Kingdom of God apart from any other religion and that was the love that they had one for another.

John 3:16 "For God so loved the world, that he gave his only begotten Son, that whosoever believeth in him should not perish, but have everlasting life."

When the Church becomes preoccupied with self, then a spiritual inversion happens and the heavens become as brass and our prayers become ineffectual.

When our focus becomes all about us, Kingdom Me, then we forget the primary reason that Jesus died on the cross.

The Kingdom of God must ever be expanding. We must never say "enough" as we push forward spreading the good news to them who do not understand it.

It does not matter what religion a person claims, because it has never been about religion. It has always been about Kingdom.

Revelation 3:14-16 "And unto the angel of the church of the Laodiceans write; These things saith the Amen, the faithful and true witness, the beginning of the creation of God; I know thy works, that thou art neither cold nor hot: I would thou wert cold or hot. So then because thou art lukewarm, and neither cold nor hot, I will spue thee out of my mouth."

Jesus does not want a lukewarm introverted church. Jesus told us to be either hot or cold, because if we ever became comfortable we would not be pressed to move forward.

Unfortunately, in many instances the body of Christ has become complacent and introverted. Our self-centered prayers have become a foul stench rising into the heavens polluting the atmosphere.

Our churches have become country clubs where people endeavor to become members and where self-help seminars are held on a weekly basis and coffee and snacks are sold in the foyer.

Our worship has become performance art and our altars have become stages. We have motivational speakers in on a regular basis and the money we invest into our own facilities far surpasses the money we send to our missionaries on the front lines.

The focus of our prayers has shifted from "Our Father who are in heaven" to "Give us this day our daily bread". Our prayers are more about our needs and desires and not about our Kings needs and desires.

The only thing that can possibly break this spiritual inversion will be a strong shaking in the body of Christ and God is preparing a perfect storm.

The Holy Spirit will come in like a mighty wind. The works of our own hands will fall to ruin and there will be a great falling away. Nevertheless the works of the Lord will stand strong throughout the tempest.

The polluted heavens will clear and we will once again be able to see the heights to which our Lord wants us to travel. Our prayers will be heard and our King will answer.

There will be many awe-inspiring signs and wonders following them who believe. The Word of God will be spoken fearlessly and there will be a great host of people added to the Kingdom of God every day.

"Kingdom Me" is about to be shaken! Many will be dismayed when the counterfeit to the Kingdom of God they have always experienced is brought to ruins.

Those who do not have their feet planted firmly on the foundation of Jesus Christ will be swept away. Those who belong to the Kingdom of God will be preserved.

CHAPTER 9

CONCLUSION

Revelation 19:11-14 "And I saw heaven opened, and behold a white horse; and he that sat upon him was called Faithful and True, and in righteousness he doth judge and make war. His eyes were as a flame of fire, and on his head were many crowns; and he had a name written, that no man knew, but he himself. And he was clothed with a vesture dipped in blood: and his name is called The Word of God. And the armies which were in heaven followed him upon white horses, clothed in fine linen, white and clean."

A storm is on the horizon and many people can see it coming. It is time to prepare for what will be a world-changing tempest.

Jesus will soon return to set up God's Millennial Kingdom based in Jerusalem. He will return with a vast army. A host of heaven made up of all those believers who have overcome death by their faith and trust in Jesus.

The world will rally together in a place called Armageddon. The combined strength of the entire world will stand against Jesus, and the combined strength of the entire world will fail.

Nothing will be able to deter Jesus from fulfilling his Father's will. No army will be able to stand before him. This day is called the Day of the Lord and the Prophet Joel describes it as a dark day and a day of blood in the following passage from Joel chapter two.

Joel 2: 1-3,11 "Blow ye the trumpet in Zion, and sound an alarm in my holy mountain: let all the inhabitants of the land tremble: for the day of the Lord cometh, for it is nigh at hand; A day of darkness and of gloominess, a day of clouds and of thick darkness, as the morning spread upon the mountains: a great people and a strong; there hath not been ever the like, neither shall be any more after it, even to the years of many generations. A fire devoureth before them; and behind them a flame burneth: the land is as the garden of Eden before them, and behind them a desolate wilderness; yea, and nothing shall escape them."

11 "And the Lord shall utter his voice before his army: for his camp is very great: for he is strong that executeth his word: for the day of the Lord is great and very terrible; and who can abide it?"

When God became man and dwelt among his people the first time he came and gave us the good news of the Kingdom of God. He came with Kingdom of God entry visas to be freely given to everyone who would believe in him and obey His commands.

He was born of a virgin, lived a sinless life, died for our sins, was buried and resurrected and ascended to the right hand of the Father where he is waiting patiently for the Father to tell him to return.

When Jesus returns, it will be with power and a burning indignation against those who spurned the gift of God and raised their fists in defiance to God. His troops will pour through the enemy ranks like water through a net. He will not stop until he has achieved his goals and he is enthroned in Jerusalem and every knee will bow and every tongue will confess that Jesus alone is Lord.

Rise up people of God and throw off your shackles and heavy yokes of religion. Rise up against the religious tyrants of our past and walk boldly forward in the light of the Kingdom of God.

Only one is deserving of our devotion, and that person is Jesus. He has shown us the way to eternal life in an everlasting Kingdom.

God will reclaim what is His own and He has given all authority to Jesus. Stand strong in the Holy Spirit during the tempest that will soon arise and precede the return of our King… Jesus.

Philippians 2:9-11 "Wherefore God also hath highly exalted him, and given him a name which is above every name: That at the name of Jesus every knee should bow, of things in heaven, and things in earth, and things under the earth; And that every tongue should confess that Jesus Christ is Lord, to the glory of God the Father."

May the blessings of God,
the Power of the Holy Spirit,
and the righteousness of our Lord Jesus Christ,
be upon all who read these words.

Bibliography

Kuhn, Thomas S. <u>The Structrue of Scientific Revolutions</u>. second.

Chicago: The University of Chigago Press, 1970.

Stern, David H. <u>The Complete Jewish Bible</u>. Jewish New

Testament Publications, Inc., 1998.